# It is Written

*It is Written*

Copyright © 2017 Rhonda Barnes. All rights reserved.

No rights claimed for public domain material, all rights reserved. No parts of this publication may be reproduced, stored in any retrieval system, or transmitted in any form or by any means, electronic, mechanical, recording, or otherwise, without the prior written permission of the author. Violations may be subject to civil or criminal penalties.

Bible Translations Used in this Book
Throughout this text, unless otherwise noted, the New King James Version is used for cited verses. When other translations are used, the following abbreviations have been applied:

AMP = Amplified Bible (Lockman Foundation 2015)
MB = Message Bible
NASU = New American Standard Updated
NLT = New Living Translation

Library of Congress Control Number: 2017939502

ISBN: 978-1-63308-263-2 (paperback)
ISBN: 978-1-63308-264-9 (ebook)

Cover & Interior Design by *R'tor John D. Maghuyop*

CHALFANT ECKERT
PUBLISHING

1028 S Bishop Avenue, Dept. 178
Rolla, MO 65401

Printed in United States of America

# It is Written

Rhonda Barnes

CHALFANT ECKERT
PUBLISHING

# DEDICATION

*It Is Written* is dedicated to my grandsons Titus, Isaac, and Brigham. May you always hide the Word of God in your hearts and may it be a light unto your path throughout all the days of your lives.

# TABLE OF CONTENTS

Introduction ................................................................... 9

| | | |
|---|---|---|
| Chapter 1 | : | THE POWER OF THE WORD ........... 15 |
| Chapter 2 | : | WHAT YOU SPEAK .............................. 19 |
| Chapter 3 | : | FAITH ................................................... 25 |
| Chapter 4 | : | PROTECTION ...................................... 33 |
| Chapter 5 | : | WARFARE ............................................. 39 |
| Chapter 6 | : | CHILDREN ........................................... 45 |
| Chapter 7 | : | SALVATION .......................................... 49 |
| Chapter 8 | : | HEALING .............................................. 53 |
| Chapter 9 | : | FINANCIAL FREEDOM ...................... 57 |
| Chapter 10 | : | NEEDS ................................................... 61 |
| Chapter 11 | : | WORSHIP/PRAISE FOR WHO HE IS ............................................. 67 |
| Chapter 12 | : | ANXIETY/FEAR/STRESS/WORRY ..... 81 |
| Chapter 13 | : | COMFORT ............................................. 89 |
| Chapter 14 | : | DEPRESSION/DISAPPOINTMENT/ DISCOURAGEMENT ........................... 95 |
| Chapter 15 | : | HOPE/PEACE/COURAGE ................ 103 |
| Chapter 16 | : | FREEDOM/LIBERTY ......................... 111 |
| Chapter 17 | : | OVERCOMING TEMPTATION AND ADDICTION ............................. 115 |
| Chapter 18 | : | ANGER ................................................ 123 |
| Chapter 19 | : | LOVE ................................................... 131 |

About the Author ......................................................... 138

# INTRODUCTION

I love the Word of God and I view it as my roadmap, my book of instructions, my inspiration and encouragement, my list of promises, my prayer guide, and a mighty weapon against the enemy (just to name a few!). We learn about the armor of God that is available to us in Ephesians Chapter 6. All of the pieces of armor are *defensive* except one – the sword of the Spirit, which is the Word of God. This is our *offensive* weapon and if we want to be victorious, we must learn how to use it wisely.

> *Finally, my brethren, be strong in the Lord and in the power of His might. Put on the whole armor of God, that you may be able to stand against the wiles of the devil. For*

*we do not wrestle against flesh and blood, but against principalities, against powers, against the rulers of the darkness of this age, against spiritual hosts of wickedness in the heavenly places. Therefore take up the whole armor of God, that you may be able to withstand in the evil day, and having done all, to stand. Stand therefore, having girded your waist with truth, having put on the breastplate of righteousness, and having shod your feet with the preparation of the gospel of peace; above all, taking the shield of faith with which you will be able to quench all the fiery darts of the wicked one. And take the helmet of salvation, and the sword of the Spirit, which is the word of God; praying always with all prayer and supplication in the Spirit, being watchful to this end with all perseverance and supplication for all the saints.*

Ephesians 6:10-18 NKJV

Speaking, proclaiming, and praying the Word of God adds great power to the life of a believer. Jesus Himself provides our greatest example. When He walked on this earth, He faced the same temptations and challenges that we as humans face. When He was led by the Spirit into the wilderness to endure a great time of testing by Satan, Jesus overcame through three words, "IT IS WRITTEN!"

*Then Jesus was led up by the Spirit into the wilderness to be tempted by the devil. And when He had fasted forty days and forty nights, afterward He was hungry. Now when the tempter came to Him, he said, "If You are the Son of God, command that these stones become bread." But He answered and said, "It is written, 'Man shall not live by bread alone, but by every word that proceeds from the mouth of God.'" Then the devil took Him up into the holy city, set Him on the pinnacle of the temple, and said to Him, "If You are the Son of God, throw Yourself down. For it is written: 'He shall give His angels charge over you,' and, 'In their hands they shall bear you up, Lest you dash your foot against a stone.'" Jesus said to him, "It is written again, 'You shall not tempt the Lord your God.'" Again, the devil took Him up on an exceedingly high mountain, and showed Him all the kingdoms of the world and their glory. And he said to Him, "All these things I will give You if You will fall down and worship me." Then Jesus said to him, "Away with you, Satan! For it is written, 'You shall worship the Lord your God, and Him only you shall serve.'" Then the devil left Him, and behold, angels came and ministered to Him.*

MATTHEW 4:1-11 NKJV

When you use the Word of God as your weapon, you also can be victorious just as Jesus was. The answer to every issue you face can be found in the pages of God's written Word. I encourage you to use these passages or create even more of your own to arm yourself and to become strong in the Lord with the power of His Word.

When you have a need, begin declaring the answer with the promises found on these pages. When you do not know what to pray, begin praying and claiming the Scriptures. Take the Word of God and write your own declarations and prayers. Hide it in your heart and you will become a mighty man or woman of faith!

CHAPTER 1

# THE POWER OF THE WORD

It is written, "For the word of God is living and active and sharper than any two-edged sword, and piercing as far as the division of soul and spirit, of both joints and marrow, and able to judge the thoughts and intentions of the heart."

Hebrews 4:12 NASU

It is written, "Forever, O Lord, Your word is settled in heaven."

Psalms 119:89 NASU

It is written, "Heaven and earth will pass away, but My words will not pass away."

Mark 13:31 NASU

It is written, "All Scripture is inspired by God and profitable for teaching, for reproof, for correction, for training in righteousness;"

2 Timothy 3:16 NASU

It is written, "So shall My word be that goes forth out of My mouth: it shall not return to Me void [without producing any effect, useless], but it shall accomplish that which I please and purpose, and it shall prosper in the thing for which I sent it."

Isaiah 55:11 AMP

It is written, "And you will know the Truth, and the Truth will set you free."

John 8:32 AMP

It is written, "Every word of God is tested; He is a shield to those who take refuge in Him."

Proverbs 30:5 NASU

It is written, "Now the parable is this: the seed is the word of God. Those beside the road are those who have heard; then the devil comes and takes away the word from their heart, so that they will not believe and be saved. Those on the rocky soil are those who, when they hear, receive the word with joy; and these have no firm root; they believe for a while, and in time of temptation fall away. The seed which fell among the thorns, these are the ones who have heard, and as they go on their way they are choked with worries and riches and pleasures of this life, and bring no fruit to maturity. But the seed in the good soil, these are the ones who have heard the word in an honest and good heart, and hold it fast, and bear fruit with perseverance."

Luke 8:11-15 NASU

It is written, "For this reason we also constantly thank God that when you received the word of God which you heard from us, you accepted it not as the word of men, but for what it really is, the word of God, which also performs its work in you who believe."

1 Thessalonians 2:13-14 NASU

It is written, "Your word is a lamp to my feet and a light to my path."

Psalm 119:105 NASU

CHAPTER 2

# What You Speak

It is written, "A good man out of the good treasure of his heart bringeth forth that which is good; and an evil man out of the evil treasure of his heart bringeth forth that which is evil: for of the abundance of the heart his mouth speaketh."

Luke 6:45 KJV

It is written, "That man shall not live by bread alone, but by every word of God."

Luke 4:4 KJV

It is written, "For we all stumble in many things. If anyone does not stumble in word, he is a perfect man, able also to bridle the whole body. Indeed, we put bits in horses' mouths that they may obey us, and we turn their whole body. Look also at ships: although they are so large and are driven by fierce winds, they are turned by a very small rudder wherever the pilot desires. Even so the tongue is a little member and boasts great things. See how great a forest a little fire kindles! And the tongue is a fire, a world of iniquity. The tongue is so set among our members that it defiles the whole body, and sets on fire the course of nature; and it is set on fire by hell. For every kind of beast and bird, of reptile and creature of the sea, is tamed and has been tamed by mankind. But no man can tame the tongue. It is an unruly evil, full of deadly poison. With it we bless our God and Father, and with it we curse men, who have been made in the similitude of God. Out of the same mouth proceed blessing and cursing. My brethren, these things ought not to be so."

James 3:2-11 NKJV

It is written, "You are snared with the words of your lips, you are caught by the speech of your mouth."

Proverbs 6:2 AMP

It is written, "Hear, for I will speak excellent and princely things; and the opening of my lips shall be for right things. For my mouth shall utter truth, and wrongdoing is detestable and loathsome to my lips."

Proverbs 8:6-7 AMP

It is written, "The wicked is [dangerously] snared by the transgression of his lips, but the [uncompromisingly] righteous shall come out of trouble. From the fruit of his words a man shall be satisfied with good, and the work of a man's hands shall come back to him [as a harvest]."

Proverbs 12:13-14 AMP

It is written, "There are those who speak rashly, like the piercing of a sword, but the tongue of the wise brings healing."

Proverbs 12:18 AMP

It is written, "Death and life are in the power of the tongue, and they who indulge in it shall eat the fruit of it [for death or life]."

Proverbs 18:21 AMP

It is written, "He who guards his mouth and his tongue keeps himself from troubles."

Proverbs 21:23 AMP

It is written, "He who guards his mouth keeps his life, but he who opens wide his lips comes to ruin."

Proverbs 13:3 AMP

"(As it is written, I have made thee a father of many nations,) before him whom he believed, even God, who quickeneth the dead, and calleth those things which be not as though they were."

Romans 4:17 KJV

It is written, "For by thy words thou shalt be justified, and by thy words thou shalt be condemned."

Matthew 12:37 KJV

# CHAPTER 3

# AITH

It is written, "And all things, whatsoever ye shall ask in prayer, believing, ye shall receive."

Matthew 21:22 KJV

It is written, "Again I say unto you, That if two of you shall agree on earth as touching any thing that they shall ask, it shall be done for them of my Father which is in heaven."

Matthew 18:19 KJV

It is written, "And Jesus answering saith unto them, Have faith in God. For verily I say unto you, That whosoever shall say unto this mountain, Be thou removed, and be thou cast into the sea; and shall not doubt in his heart, but shall believe that those things which he saith shall come to pass; he shall have whatsoever he saith. Therefore I say unto you, What things soever ye desire, when ye pray, believe that ye receive them, and ye shall have them."

Mark 11:22-24 KJV


It is written, "Jesus said unto him, If thou canst believe, all things are possible to him that believeth."

Mark 9:23 KJV


It is written, "And these signs shall follow them that believe; In my name shall they cast out devils; they shall speak with new tongues; They shall take up serpents; and if they drink any deadly thing, it shall not hurt them; they shall lay hands on the sick, and they shall recover."

Mark 16:17-18 KJV

It is written, "Truly, truly, I say to you, he who believes in Me, the works that I do, he will do also; and greater works than these he will do; because I go to the Father. Whatever you ask in My name, that will I do, so that the Father may be glorified in the Son. If you ask Me anything in My name, I will do it."

John 14:12-14 NASU

It is written, "Truly, truly, I say to you, if you ask the Father for anything in My name, He will give it to you. Until now you have asked for nothing in My name; ask and you will receive, so that your joy may be made full."

John 16:23-24 NASU

It is written, "If you abide in Me, and My words abide in you, ask whatever you wish, and it will be done for you."

John 15:7 NASU

It is written, "Consider it all joy, my brethren, when you encounter various trials, knowing that the testing of your faith produces endurance. And let endurance have its perfect result, so that you may be perfect and complete, lacking in nothing. But if any of you lacks wisdom, let him ask of God, who gives to all generously and without reproach, and it will be given to him. But he must ask in faith without any doubting, for the one who doubts is like the surf of the sea, driven and tossed by the wind. For that man ought not to expect that he will receive anything from the Lord, being a double-minded man, unstable in all his ways."

JAMES 1:2-8 NASU


It is written, "Is anyone among you sick? He should call in the church elders (the spiritual guides). And they should pray over him, anointing him with oil in the Lord's name. And the prayer [that is] of faith will save him who is sick, and the Lord will restore him; and if he has committed sins, he will be forgiven. Confess to one another therefore your faults (your slips, your false steps, your offenses, your sins) and pray [also] for one another, that you may be healed and restored [to a spiritual tone of mind and heart]. The earnest (heartfelt, continued) prayer of a righteous man makes tremendous power available [dynamic in its working]."

James 5:14-16 AMP

It is written, "So faith comes from hearing, and hearing by the word of Christ."

Romans 10:17 NASU

It is written, "For in it the righteousness of God is revealed from faith to faith; as it is written, 'BUT THE RIGHTEOUS man SHALL LIVE BY FAITH.'"

Romans 1:17 NASU

It is written, "For whatever is born of God is victorious over the world; and this is the victory that conquers the world, even our faith."

1 John 5:4 AMP

It is written, "This is the confidence which we have before Him, that, if we ask anything according to His will, He hears us."

1 John 5:14 NASU

It is written, "Let us hold fast the profession of our faith without wavering; (for he is faithful that promised;)"

Hebrews 10:23 KJV

It is written, "Now faith is the substance of things hoped for, the evidence of things not seen."

Hebrews 11:1 KJV

It is written, "My soul, wait only upon God and silently submit to Him; for my hope and expectation are from Him."

Psalms 62:5 AMP


It is written, "And when I came to you, brethren, I did not come with superiority of speech or of wisdom, proclaiming to you the testimony of God.... and my message and my preaching were not in persuasive words of wisdom, but in demonstration of the Spirit and of power, so that your faith would not rest on the wisdom of men, but on the power of God."

1 Corinthians 2:1, 2:4-5 NASU


It is written, "But having the same spirit of faith, according to what is written, 'I BELIEVED, THEREFORE I SPOKE,' we also believe, therefore we also speak,"

2 Corinthians 4:13 NASU

It is written, "For we walk by faith, not by sight."

2 CORINTHIANS 5:7 NASU

# CHAPTER 4

# PROTECTION

It is written, "HE WHO dwells in the secret place of the Most High shall remain stable and fixed under the shadow of the Almighty [Whose power no foe can withstand]. I will say of the Lord, He is my Refuge and my Fortress, my God; on Him I lean and rely, and in Him I [confidently] trust! For [then] He will deliver you from the snare of the fowler and from the deadly pestilence. [Then] He will cover you with His pinions, and under His wings shall you trust and find refuge; His truth and His faithfulness are a shield and a buckler. You shall not be afraid of the terror of the night, nor of the arrow (the evil plots and slanders of the wicked) that flies by day, Nor of the pestilence that stalks in darkness, nor of the destruction and sudden death that surprise and lay waste at noonday. A thousand may fall at your side, and ten thousand at your right hand, but it shall not come near you. Only a spectator shall you be [yourself inaccessible in the secret place of the Most High] as you witness the reward of the wicked. Because you have made the Lord your refuge, and the Most High your dwelling place, There shall no evil befall you, nor any plague or calamity come near your tent. For He will give His angels [especial] charge over you to accompany and defend and preserve you in all your ways [of obedience and service]."

Psalms 91:1-11 AMP

It is written, "I will lift up my eyes to the hills from whence comes my help? My help comes from the Lord, Who made heaven and earth. He will not allow your foot to be moved; He who keeps you will not slumber. Behold, He who keeps Israel shall neither slumber nor sleep. The Lord is your keeper; The Lord is your shade at your right hand. The sun shall not strike you by day, nor the moon by night. The Lord shall preserve you from all evil; He shall preserve your soul. The Lord shall preserve your going out and your coming in from this time forth, and even forevermore."

Psalm 121:1-8 NKJV

It is written, "The Lord is a shelter for the oppressed, a refuge in times of trouble. Those who know your name trust in you, for you, O Lord, do not abandon those who search for you."

Psalm 9:9-10 NLT

It is written, "But the Lord is faithful, and He will strengthen and protect you from the evil one."

2 Thessalonians 3:3-4 NASU

It is written, "But Moses told the people, 'Don't be afraid. Just stand still and watch the Lord rescue you today. The Egyptians you see today will never be seen again. The Lord himself will fight for you. Just stay calm.'"

Exodus 14:13-14 NLT

It is written, "For the Lord God is a Sun and Shield; the Lord bestows [present] grace and favor and [future] glory (honor, splendor, and heavenly bliss)! No good thing will He withhold from those who walk uprightly."

Psalm 84:11 AMP

It is written, "God is our refuge and strength, a very present help in trouble. Therefore we will not fear, though the earth should change and though the mountains slip into the heart of the sea;"

Psalm 46:1-2 NASU

It is written, "The Lord is my light and my salvation; whom shall I fear? The Lord is the defense of my life; whom shall I dread?"

Psalm 27:1 NASU

# CHAPTER 5

# WARFARE

It is written, "For though we walk (live) in the flesh, we are not carrying on our warfare according to the flesh and using mere human weapons. For the weapons of our warfare are not physical [weapons of flesh and blood], but they are mighty before God for the overthrow and destruction of strongholds, [Inasmuch as we] refute arguments and theories and reasonings and every proud and lofty thing that sets itself up against the [true] knowledge of God; and we lead every thought and purpose away captive into the obedience of Christ (the Messiah, the Anointed One),"

2 Corinthians 10:3-5 AMP

It is written, "Put on God's whole armor [the armor of a heavy-armed soldier which God supplies], that you may be able successfully to stand up against [all] the strategies and the deceits of the devil. For we are not wrestling with flesh and blood [contending only with physical opponents], but against the despotisms, against the powers, against [the master spirits who are] the world rulers of this present darkness, against the spirit forces of wickedness in the heavenly (supernatural) sphere. Therefore put on God's complete armor, that you may be able to resist and stand your ground on the evil day [of danger], and, having done all [the crisis demands], to stand [firmly in your place]. Stand therefore [hold your ground], having tightened the belt of truth around your loins and having put on the breastplate of integrity and of moral rectitude and right standing with God, And having shod your feet in preparation [to face the enemy with the firm-footed stability, the promptness, and the readiness produced by the good news] of the Gospel of peace. Lift up over all the [covering] shield of saving faith, upon which you can quench all the flaming missiles of the wicked [one]. And take the helmet of salvation and the sword that the Spirit wields, which is the Word of God. Pray at all times (on every occasion, in every season) in the Spirit, with all [manner of] prayer and entreaty. To that end keep alert and watch with strong purpose and perseverance, interceding in behalf of all the saints (God's consecrated people)."

Ephesians 6:11-18 AMP

It is written, "Then I heard a loud voice in heaven, saying, "Now the salvation, and the power, and the kingdom of our God and the authority of His Christ have come, for the accuser of our brethren has been thrown down, he who accuses them before our God day and night. And they overcame him because of the blood of the Lamb and because of the word of their testimony,"

Revelation 12:10-11 NASU

It is written, "The thief comes only in order to steal and kill and destroy. I came that they may have and enjoy life, and have it in abundance (to the full, till it overflows)."

John 10:10 AMP

It is written, "The one who practices sin is of the devil; for the devil has sinned from the beginning. The Son of God appeared for this purpose, to destroy the works of the devil."

1 John 3:8-9 NASU

It is written, "So be subject to God. Resist the devil [stand firm against him], and he will flee from you."

James 4:7 AMP

It is written, "Five of you will chase a hundred, and a hundred of you will chase ten thousand, and your enemies will fall before you by the sword."

Leviticus 26:8-9 NASU

It is written, "One of your men puts to flight a thousand, for the Lord your God is He who fights for you, just as He promised you."

JOSHUA 23:10-11 NASU

# CHAPTER 6

# CHILDREN

It is written, "Train up a child in the way he should go, even when he is old he will not depart from it."

Proverbs 22:6 NASU

It is written, "Fathers, do not provoke your children to anger, but bring them up in the discipline and instruction of the Lord."

Ephesians 6:4 NASU

It is written, "Praise the Lord! How joyful are those who fear the Lord and delight in obeying his commands. Their children will be successful everywhere; an entire generation of godly people will be blessed. They themselves will be wealthy, and their good deeds will last forever. Light shines in the darkness for the godly. They are generous, compassionate, and righteous. Good comes to those who lend money generously and conduct their business fairly. Such people will not be overcome by evil. Those who are righteous will be long remembered. They do not fear bad news; they confidently trust the Lord to care for them. They are confident and fearless and can face their foes triumphantly. They share freely and give generously to those in need. Their good deeds will be remembered forever. They will have influence and honor."

PSALMS 112:1-9 NLT


It is written, "The just man walketh in his integrity: his children are blessed after him."

PROVERBS 20:7 KJV

It is written, "Behold, children are a gift of the Lord, the fruit of the womb is a reward. Like arrows in the hand of a warrior, so are the children of one's youth. How blessed is the man whose quiver is full of them;"

PSALM 127:3-5A NASU

It is written, "Grandchildren are the crowning glory of the aged; parents are the pride of their children."

PROVERBS 17:6 NLT

It is written, "The father of godly children has cause for joy. What a pleasure to have children who are wise."

PROVERBS 23:24 NLT

It is written, "All your children shall be taught by the Lord, and great shall be the peace of your children."

ISAIAH 54:13 NKJV

# CHAPTER 7

# SALVATION

It is written, "Believe in the Lord Jesus and you will be saved, along with everyone in your household."

ACTS 16:31 NLT

It is written, "The Lord is not slow about His promise, as some count slowness, but is patient toward you, not wishing for any to perish but for all to come to repentance."

2 PETER 3:9 NASU

It is written, "Blessed is a man who perseveres under trial; for once he has been approved, he will receive the crown of life which the Lord has promised to those who love Him."

James 1:12-13 NASU

"As it is written, None is righteous, just and truthful and upright and conscientious, no, not one. Since all have sinned and are falling short of the honor and glory which God bestows and receives. Therefore, as sin came into the world through one man, and death as the result of sin, so death spread to all men, [no one being able to stop it or to escape its power] because all men sinned. But God shows and clearly proves His [own] love for us by the fact that while we were still sinners, Christ (the Messiah, the Anointed One) died for us."

Romans 3:10; 23; 5:12; 8 AMP

It is written, "For by grace you have been saved through faith; and that not of yourselves, it is the gift of God; not as a result of works, so that no one may boast."

Ephesians 2:8-9 NASU

It is written, "Therefore there is now no condemnation for those who are in Christ Jesus. For the law of the Spirit of life in Christ Jesus has set you free from the law of sin and of death."

Romans 8:1-2 NASU

It is written, "Peter said to them, 'Repent, and each of you be baptized in the name of Jesus Christ for the forgiveness of your sins; and you will receive the gift of the Holy Spirit.'"

Acts 2:38-39 NASU

It is written, "For this is My blood of the covenant, which is poured out for many for forgiveness of sins."

Matthew 26:28 NASU

It is written, "And My people who are called by My name humble themselves and pray and seek My face and turn from their wicked ways, then I will hear from heaven, will forgive their sin and will heal their land."

2 Chronicles 7:14 NASU

It is written, "And it shall come to pass that whoever calls on the name of the Lord shall be saved."

Joel 2:32 NKJV

It is written, "I, even I, am He Who blots out and cancels your transgressions, for My own sake, and I will not remember your sins."

Isaiah 43:25 AMP

# CHAPTER 8

# Healing

It is written, "Who his own self bare our sins in his own body on the tree, that we, being dead to sins, should live unto righteousness: by whose stripes ye were healed."

1 Peter 2:24 KJV

It is written, "Bless the Lord, O my soul, And forget none of His benefits; Who pardons all your iniquities, Who heals all your diseases;"

Psalms 103:2-3 NASU

It is written, "Surely He has borne our griefs And carried our sorrows; Yet we esteemed Him stricken, Smitten by God, and afflicted. But He was wounded for our transgressions, He was bruised for our iniquities; The chastisement for our peace was upon Him, And by His stripes we are healed."

Isaiah 53:4-5 NKJV

It is written, "My son, attend to my words; consent and submit to my sayings. Let them not depart from your sight; keep them in the center of your heart. For they are life to those who find them, healing and health to all their flesh."

Proverbs 4:20-22 AMP

It is written, "Saying, If you will diligently hearken to the voice of the Lord your God and will do what is right in His sight, and will listen to and obey His commandments and keep all His statutes, I will put none of the diseases upon you which I brought upon the Egyptians, for I am the Lord Who heals you."

Exodus 15:26 AMP

It is written, "Then they cry to the Lord in their trouble, and He delivers them out of their distresses. He sends forth His word and heals them and rescues them from the pit and destruction."

PSALMS 107:19-20 AMP

It is written, "And thus He fulfilled what was spoken by the prophet Isaiah, He Himself took [in order to carry away] our weaknesses and infirmities and bore away our diseases."

MATTHEW 8:17 AMP

It is written, "You were bought with a price [purchased with a preciousness and paid for, made His own]. So then, honor God and bring glory to Him in your body."

1 CORINTHIANS 6:20 AMP

# CHAPTER 9

# FINANCIAL FREEDOM

It is written, "But seek (aim at and strive after) first of all His kingdom and His righteousness (His way of doing and being right), and then all these things taken together will be given you besides."

MATTHEW 6:33 AMP

It is written, "And my God will liberally supply (fill to the full) your every need according to His riches in glory in Christ Jesus."

PHILIPPIANS 4:19 AMP

It is written, "Bring all the tithes (the whole tenth of your income) into the storehouse, that there may be food in My house, and prove Me now by it, says the Lord of hosts, if I will not open the windows of heaven for you and pour you out a blessing, that there shall not be room enough to receive it."

Malachi 3:10 AMP

It is written, "Honor the Lord with your capital and sufficiency [from righteous labors] and with the firstfruits of all your income; So shall your storage places be filled with plenty, and your vats shall be overflowing with new wine."

Proverbs 3:9-10 AMP

It is written, "This I say, he who sows sparingly will also reap sparingly, and he who sows bountifully will also reap bountifully. Each one must do just as he has purposed in his heart, not grudgingly or under compulsion, for God loves a cheerful giver. And God is able to make all grace abound to you, so that always having all sufficiency in everything, you may have an abundance for every good deed; as it is written, 'HE SCATTERED ABROAD, HE GAVE TO THE POOR, HIS RIGHTEOUSNESS ENDURES FOREVER.' Now He who supplies seed to the sower and bread for food will supply and multiply your seed for sowing and increase the harvest of your righteousness; you will be enriched in everything for all liberality, which through us is producing thanksgiving to God."

2 Corinthians 9:6-12 NASU

It is written, "As for the rich in this world, charge them not to be proud and arrogant and contemptuous of others, nor to set their hopes on uncertain riches, but on God, Who richly and ceaselessly provides us with everything for [our] enjoyment."

1 Timothy 6:17 AMP

It is written, "Give, and it will be given to you. They will pour into your lap a good measure — pressed down, shaken together, and running over. For by your standard of measure it will be measured to you in return."

Luke 6:38 NASU

It is written, "This Book of the Law shall not depart out of your mouth, but you shall meditate on it day and night, that you may observe and do according to all that is written in it. For then you shall make your way prosperous, and then you shall deal wisely and have good success."

Joshua 1:8 AMP

# CHAPTER 10

# Needs

It is written, "And when you are praying, do not use meaningless repetition as the Gentiles do, for they suppose that they will be heard for their many words. So do not be like them; for your Father knows what you need before you ask Him."

Matthew 6:7-8 NASU

It is written, "The young lions lack food and suffer hunger, but they who seek (inquire of and require) the Lord [by right of their need and on the authority of His Word], none of them shall lack any beneficial thing."

Psalms 34:10 AMP

It is written, "Ask, and it will be given to you; seek, and you will find; knock, and it will be opened to you. For everyone who asks receives, and he who seeks finds, and to him who knocks it will be opened."

MATTHEW 7:7-8 NASU

It is written, "He who did not spare His own Son, but delivered Him over for us all, how will He not also with Him freely give us all things?"

ROMANS 8:32 NASU

It is written, "Commit your way to the Lord [roll and repose each care of your load on Him]; trust (lean on, rely on, and be confident) also in Him and He will bring it to pass."

PSALMS 37:5 AMP

It is written, "Now to Him who is able to do far more abundantly beyond all that we ask or think, according to the power that works within us,"

> EPHESIANS 3:20 NASU

It is written, "Grace and peace be multiplied to you in the knowledge of God and of Jesus our Lord; seeing that His divine power has granted to us everything pertaining to life and godliness, through the true knowledge of Him who called us by His own glory and excellence."

> 2 PETER 1:2-4 NASU

It is written, "Call to Me and I will answer you, and I will tell you great and mighty things, which you do not know."

> JEREMIAH 33:3 NASU

It is written, "Behold, I am the Lord, the God of all flesh; is anything too difficult for Me?"

> JEREMIAH 32:27 NASU

It is written, "Come to Me, all who are weary and heavy-laden, and I will give you rest. Take My yoke upon you and learn from Me, for I am gentle and humble in heart, and YOU WILL FIND REST FOR YOUR SOULS. For My yoke is easy and My burden is light."

Matthew 11:28-30 NASU

It is written, "For he hath said, I will never leave thee, nor forsake thee."

Hebrews 13:5 KJV

It is written, "Be anxious for nothing, but in everything by prayer and supplication with thanksgiving let your requests be made known to God. And the peace of God, which surpasses all comprehension, will guard your hearts and your minds in Christ Jesus."

Philippians 4:6-7 NASU

It is written, "May He grant you according to your heart's desire and fulfill all your plans."

PSALMS 20:4 AMP

It is written, "Blessed be the God and Father of our Lord Jesus Christ, who has blessed us with every spiritual blessing in the heavenly places in Christ,"

EPHESIANS 1:3 NASU

It is written, "THE LORD is my Shepherd [to feed, guide, and shield me], I shall not lack. He makes me lie down in [fresh, tender] green pastures; He leads me beside the still and restful waters. He refreshes and restores my life (my self); He leads me in the paths of righteousness [uprightness and right standing with Him — not for my earning it, but] for His name's sake."

PSALM 23:1-3 AMP

It is written, "But seek His kingdom, and these things will be added to you. Do not be afraid, little flock, for your Father has chosen gladly to give you the kingdom."

Luke 12:31-32 NASU

CHAPTER 11

# Worship/ Praise for Who He Is

It is written, "For to us a Child is born, to us a Son is given; and the government shall be upon His shoulder, and His name shall be called Wonderful Counselor, Mighty God, Everlasting Father [of Eternity], Prince of Peace."

Isaiah 9:6 AMP

It is written, "Behold, He is coming with the clouds, and every eye will see Him, even those who pierced Him; and all the tribes of the earth shall gaze upon Him and beat their breasts and mourn and lament over Him. Even so [must it be]. Amen (so be it). I am the Alpha and the Omega, the Beginning and the End, says the Lord God, He Who is and Who was and Who is to come, the Almighty (the Ruler of all)."

Revelation 1:7-8 AMP

It is written, "For there [is only] one God, and [only] one Mediator between God and men, the Man Christ Jesus,"

1 Timothy 2:5 AMP

It is written, "The Lord is my shepherd, I shall not want. He makes me lie down in green pastures; He leads me beside quiet waters. He restores my soul; He guides me in the paths of righteousness For His name's sake."

Psalms 23:1-3 NASU

It is written, "Now to the King eternal, immortal, invisible, the only God, be honor and glory forever and ever. Amen."

1 Timothy 1:17 NASU

It is written, "Jesus said to him, 'I am the way, and the truth, and the life; no one comes to the Father but through Me.'"

John 14:6 NASU

It is written, "That men may know that thou, whose name alone is JEHOVAH, art the most high over all the earth."

Psalms 83:18 KJV

It is written, "Behold, God, my salvation! I will trust and not be afraid, for the Lord God is my strength and song; yes, He has become my salvation. Therefore with joy will you draw water from the wells of salvation. And in that day you will say, Give thanks to the

Lord, call upon His name and by means of His name [in solemn entreaty]; declare and make known His deeds among the peoples of the earth, proclaim that His name is exalted! Sing praises to the Lord, for He has done excellent things [gloriously]; let this be made known to all the earth. Cry aloud and shout joyfully, you women and inhabitants of Zion, for great in your midst is the Holy One of Israel."

Isaiah 12:2-6 AMP


It is written, "HOW LOVELY are Your tabernacles, O Lord of hosts! My soul yearns, yes, even pines and is homesick for the courts of the Lord; my heart and my flesh cry out and sing for joy to the living God. Yes, the sparrow has found a house, and the swallow a nest for herself, where she may lay her young — even Your altars, O Lord of hosts, my King and my God. Blessed (happy, fortunate, to be envied) are those who dwell in Your house and Your presence; they will be singing Your praises all the day long. Selah [pause, and calmly think of that]! Blessed (happy, fortunate, to be envied) is the man whose strength is in You, in whose heart are the highways to Zion. Passing through the Valley of Weeping (Baca), they make it a place of springs; the early rain also fills [the pools] with blessings. They go from strength to strength [increasing in victorious power]; each of them appears before God in Zion. O Lord God of hosts, hear my prayer; give ear, O God of Jacob! Selah [pause, and calmly think of that]! Behold our shield [the king as Your agent], O God, and look upon the face of Your anointed! For a day in Your courts is better than a thousand [anywhere else]; I would rather be a doorkeeper and stand at the threshold in the house of my God than to dwell [at ease] in the tents of wickedness. For the Lord God is a Sun and Shield; the Lord bestows [present] grace and favor and [future] glory (honor, splendor, and heavenly bliss)! No good thing will He withhold from those who walk uprightly. O Lord of hosts, blessed (happy, fortunate, to be envied) is the man who trusts in You [leaning and believing on

You, committing all and confidently looking to You, and that without fear or misgiving]!"

Psalms 84 AMP

It is written, "Trust ye in the Lord for ever: for in the Lord JEHOVAH is everlasting strength:"

Isaiah 26:4 KJV

It is written, "O give thanks to the Lord, call on His name; make known His doings among the peoples! Sing to Him, sing praises to Him; meditate on and talk of all His wondrous works and devoutly praise them! Glory in His holy name; let the hearts of those rejoice who seek the Lord! Seek the Lord and His strength; yearn for and seek His face and to be in His presence continually!"

1 Chronicles 16:8-11 AMP

It is written, "Yours, O Lord, is the greatness and the power and the glory and the victory and the majesty, for all that is in the heavens and the earth is Yours; Yours is the kingdom, O Lord, and Yours it is to be exalted as Head over all. Both riches and honor come from You, and You reign over all. In Your hands are power and might; in Your hands it is to make great and to give strength to all. Now therefore, our God, we thank You and praise Your glorious name and those attributes which that name denotes."

1 Chronicles 29:11-13 AMP

It is written, "I WILL praise You, O Lord, with my whole heart; I will show forth (recount and tell aloud) all Your marvelous works and wonderful deeds! I will rejoice in You and be in high spirits; I will sing praise to Your name, O Most High!"

Psalms 9:1-2 AMP

It is written, "The Lord is my Strength and my [impenetrable] Shield; my heart trusts in, relies on, and confidently leans on Him, and I am helped; therefore my heart greatly rejoices, and with my song will I praise Him. The Lord is their [unyielding] Strength, and He is the Stronghold of salvation to [me] His anointed."

Psalms 28:7-8 AMP

It is written, "I WILL bless the Lord at all times; His praise shall continually be in my mouth. My life makes its boast in the Lord; let the humble and afflicted hear and be glad. O magnify the Lord with me, and let us exalt His name together. I sought (inquired of) the Lord and required Him [of necessity and on the authority of His Word], and He heard me, and delivered me from all my fears."

Psalms 34:1-4 AMP

It is written, "I will praise and give thanks to You, O Lord, among the peoples; I will sing praises to You among the nations. For Your mercy and loving-kindness are great, reaching to the heavens, and Your truth and faithfulness to the clouds. Be exalted, O God, above the heavens; let Your glory be over all the earth."

Psalms 57:9-11 AMP

It is written, "Because Your loving-kindness is better than life, my lips shall praise You. So will I bless You while I live; I will lift up my hands in Your name. My whole being shall be satisfied as with marrow and fatness; and my mouth shall praise You with joyful lips When I remember You upon my bed and meditate on You in the night watches. For You have been my help, and in the shadow of Your wings will I rejoice. My whole being follows hard after You and clings closely to You; Your right hand upholds me."

Psalms 63:3-8 AMP

It is written, "MAKE A joyful noise unto God, all the earth; Sing forth the honor and glory of His name; make His praise glorious! Say to God, How awesome and fearfully glorious are Your works! Through the greatness of Your power shall Your enemies submit themselves to You [with feigned and reluctant obedience]. All the earth shall bow down to You and sing [praises] to You; they shall praise Your name in song. Selah [pause, and calmly think of that]!"

Psalms 66:1-4 AMP

It is written, "My praise is continually of You. I am as a wonder and surprise to many, but You are my strong refuge. My mouth shall be filled with Your praise and with Your honor all the day."

Psalms 71:6-8 AMP

It is written, "PRAISE THE Lord! (Hallelujah!) I will praise and give thanks to the Lord with my whole heart in the council of the upright and in the congregation. The works of the Lord are great, sought out by all those who have delight in them. His work is honorable and glorious, and His righteousness endures forever. He has made His wonderful works to be remembered; the Lord is gracious, merciful, and full of loving compassion."

Psalms 111:1-4 AMP

It is written, "I WILL extol You, my God, O King; and I will bless Your name forever and ever [with grateful, affectionate praise]. Every day [with its new reasons] will I bless You [affectionately and gratefully praise You]; yes, I will praise Your name forever and ever. Great is the Lord and highly to be praised; and His greatness is [so vast and deep as to be] unsearchable. One generation shall laud Your works to another and shall declare Your mighty acts. On the glorious splendor of Your majesty and on Your wondrous works I will meditate. Men shall speak of the might of Your tremendous and terrible acts, and I will declare

Your greatness. They shall pour forth [like a fountain] the fame of Your great and abundant goodness and shall sing aloud of Your rightness and justice. The Lord is gracious and full of compassion, slow to anger and abounding in mercy and loving-kindness. The Lord is good to all, and His tender mercies are over all His works [the entirety of things created]. All Your works shall praise You, O Lord, and Your loving ones shall bless You [affectionately and gratefully shall Your saints confess and praise You]! They shall speak of the glory of Your kingdom and talk of Your power, To make known to the sons of men God's mighty deeds and the glorious majesty of His kingdom. Your kingdom is an everlasting kingdom, and Your dominion endures throughout all generations. The Lord upholds all those [of His own] who are falling and raises up all those who are bowed down. The eyes of all wait for You [looking, watching, and expecting] and You give them their food in due season. You open Your hand and satisfy every living thing with favor. The Lord is [rigidly] righteous in all

His ways and gracious and merciful in all His works. The Lord is near to all who call upon Him, to all who call upon Him sincerely and in truth. He will fulfill the desires of those who reverently and worshipfully fear Him; He also will hear their cry and will save them. The Lord preserves all those who love Him, but all the wicked will He destroy. My mouth shall speak the praise of the Lord; and let all flesh bless (affectionately and gratefully praise) His holy name forever and ever."

Psalms 145 AMP

CHAPTER 12

# *A*NXIETY/FEAR/ STRESS/WORRY

It is written, "In the day of my trouble I will call upon You, for You will answer me."

PSALM 86:7 NKJV

It is written, "And who of you by being worried can add a single hour to his life? And why are you worried about clothing? Observe how the lilies of the field grow; they do not toil nor do they spin, yet I say to you that not even Solomon in all his glory clothed himself like one of these. But if God so clothes the grass of the field, which is alive today and tomorrow is thrown into the furnace, will He not much more clothe you? You of little faith! Do not worry then, saying, 'What will we eat?' or 'What will we drink?' or 'What will we wear for clothing?' For the Gentiles eagerly seek all these things; for your heavenly Father knows that you need all these things. But seek first His kingdom and His righteousness, and all these things will be added to you. So do not worry about tomorrow; for tomorrow will care for itself. Each day has enough trouble of its own."

MATTHEW 6:27-34 NASU


It is written, "Do not fear, for I am with you; do not anxiously look about you, for I am your God. I will strengthen you, surely I will help you, surely I will uphold you with My righteous right hand."

ISAIAH 41:10 NASU

It is written, "Be anxious for nothing, but in everything by prayer and supplication with thanksgiving let your requests be made known to God."

Philippians 4:6 NASU

It is written, "Casting the whole of your care [all your anxieties, all your worries, all your concerns, once and for all] on Him, for He cares for you affectionately and cares about you watchfully."

1 Peter 5:7 AMP

It is written, "Cast your burden on the Lord [releasing the weight of it] and He will sustain you; He will never allow the [consistently] righteous to be moved (made to slip, fall, or fail)."

Psalm 55:22 AMP

It is written, "Search me, O God, and know my heart; try me and know my anxious thoughts; and see if there be any hurtful way in me, and lead me in the everlasting way."

Psalm 139:23-24 NASU

It is written, "All the days of the desponding and afflicted are made evil [by anxious thoughts and forebodings], but he who has a glad heart has a continual feast [regardless of circumstances]."

Proverbs 15:15 AMP

It is written, "Then the cares and anxieties of the world and distractions of the age, and the pleasure and delight and false glamour and deceitfulness of riches, and the craving and passionate desire for other things creep in and choke and suffocate the Word, and it becomes fruitless."

Mark 4:19 AMP

It is written, "GOD IS our Refuge and Strength [mighty and impenetrable to temptation], a very present and well-proved help in trouble. Therefore we will not fear, though the earth should change and though the mountains be shaken into the midst of the seas,"

Psalm 46:1-2 AMP

It is written, "For God has not given us a spirit of fear, but of power and of love and of a sound mind."

2 Timothy 1:7 NKJV

It is written, "The Lord is my light and my salvation; whom shall I fear? The Lord is the strength of my life; of whom shall I be afraid?"

Psalm 27:1 NKJV

It is written, "Do not let your heart be troubled; believe in God, believe also in Me."

John 14:1 NASU

It is written, "So you have not received a spirit that makes you fearful slaves. Instead, you received God's Spirit when he adopted you as his own children. Now we call him, Abba, Father."

Romans 8:15 NLT

It is written, "There is no fear in love [dread does not exist], but full-grown (complete, perfect) love turns fear out of doors and expels every trace of terror! For fear brings with it the thought of punishment, and [so] he who is afraid has not reached the full maturity of love [is not yet grown into love's complete perfection]. We love Him, because He first loved us."

1 John 4:18-19 AMP

It is written, "Do not be afraid of sudden fear nor of the onslaught of the wicked when it comes; for the Lord will be your confidence and will keep your foot from being caught"

Proverbs 3:25-26 NASU

It is written, "In God I have put my trust, I shall not be afraid. What can man do to me?"

Psalm 56:11 NASU

It is written, "Even though I walk through the valley of the shadow of death, I fear no evil, for You are with me; Your rod and Your staff, they comfort me. You prepare a table before me in the presence of my enemies; You have anointed my head with oil; My cup overflows. Surely goodness and lovingkindness will follow me all the days of my life, and I will dwell in the house of the Lord forever."

Psalm 23:4-6 NASU

It is written, "So we take comfort and are encouraged and confidently and boldly say, The Lord is my Helper; I will not be seized with alarm [I will not fear or dread or be terrified]. What can man do to me?"

Hebrews 13:6 AMP

It is written, "The Lord is for me; I will not fear; what can man do to me?"

> PSALM 118:6 NASU

# CHAPTER 13

# Comfort

It is written, "Blessed are those who mourn, for they shall be comforted."

MATTHEW 5:4 NASU

It is written, "The Lord is near to the brokenhearted and saves those who are crushed in spirit. Many are the afflictions of the righteous, but the Lord delivers him out of them all."

PSALM 34:18-19 NASU

It is written, "Even though I walk through the valley of the shadow of death, I fear no evil, for

You are with me; Your rod and Your staff, they comfort me."

Psalm 23:4 NASU

It is written, "Weeping may endure for a night, but joy comes in the morning."

Psalm 30:5b AMP

It is written, "For our light, momentary affliction (this slight distress of the passing hour) is ever more and more abundantly preparing and producing and achieving for us an everlasting weight of glory [beyond all measure, excessively surpassing all comparisons and all calculations, a vast and transcendent glory and blessedness never to cease!], since we consider and look not to the things that are seen but to the things that are unseen; for the things that are visible are temporal (brief and fleeting), but the things that are invisible are deathless and everlasting."

2 Corinthians 4:17-18 AMP

It is written, "He heals the brokenhearted, and binds up their wounds."

Psalm 147:3 NASU

It is written, "Remember the word to Your servant, in which You have made me hope. This is my comfort in my affliction, that Your word has revived me. I have remembered Your ordinances from of old, O Lord, and comfort myself."

Psalm 119:49-50; 52 NASU

It is written, "Blessed be the God and Father of our Lord Jesus Christ, the Father of mercies and God of all comfort, who comforts us in all our affliction so that we will be able to comfort those who are in any affliction with the comfort with which we ourselves are comforted by God. For just as the sufferings of Christ are ours in abundance, so also our comfort is abundant through Christ."

2 Corinthians 1:3-5 NASU

It is written, "I will lift up my eyes to the mountains; from where shall my help come? My help comes from the Lord, Who made heaven and earth. He will not allow your foot to slip; He who keeps you will not slumber."

Psalm 121:1-3 NASU

It is written, "For the Lord Himself will descend from heaven with a shout, with the voice of the archangel and with the trumpet of God, and the dead in Christ will rise first. Then we who are alive and remain will be caught up together with them in the clouds to meet the Lord in the air, and so we shall always be with the Lord. Therefore comfort one another with these words."

1 Thessalonians 4:16-18 NASU

It is written, "Now may our Lord Jesus Christ Himself and God our Father, who has loved us and given us eternal comfort and good hope by grace, comfort and strengthen your hearts in every good work and word."

2 Thessalonians 2:16-17 NASU

CHAPTER 14

# DEPRESSION/ DISAPPOINTMENT/ DISCOURAGEMENT

It is written, "And let us not lose heart and grow weary and faint in acting nobly and doing right, for in due time and at the appointed season we shall reap, if we do not loosen and relax our courage and faint."

GALATIANS 6:9 AMP

It is written, "Come to Me, all who are weary and heavy-laden, and I will give you rest. Take My yoke upon you and learn from Me, for I am gentle and humble in heart, and YOU

WILL FIND REST FOR YOUR SOULS. For My yoke is easy and My burden is light."

Matthew 11:28-30 NASU

It is written, "Why are you cast down, O my inner self? And why should you moan over me and be disquieted within me? Hope in God and wait expectantly for Him, for I shall yet praise Him, my Help and my God."

Psalm 42:5 AMP

It is written, "So the ransomed of the Lord shall return, and come to Zion with singing, with everlasting joy on their heads. They shall obtain joy and gladness; sorrow and sighing shall flee away."

Isaiah 51:11 NKJV

It is written, "Be anxious for nothing, but in everything by prayer and supplication with thanksgiving let your requests be made known to God. And the peace of God, which surpasses all comprehension, will guard your hearts and your minds in Christ Jesus. Finally, brethren, whatever is true, whatever is honorable, whatever is right, whatever is pure, whatever is lovely, whatever is of good repute, if there is any excellence and if anything worthy of praise, dwell on these things. The things you have learned and received and heard and seen in me, practice these things, and the God of peace will be with you."

Philippians 4:6-9 NASU

It is written, "We are hard-pressed on every side, yet not crushed; we are perplexed, but not in despair; persecuted, but not forsaken; struck down, but not destroyed."

2 Corinthians 4:8-9 NKJV

It is written, "Therefore, do not throw away your confidence, which has a great reward. For you have need of endurance, so that when you have done the will of God, you may receive what was promised."

Hebrews 10:35-36 NASU

It is written, "For I am confident of this very thing, that He who began a good work in you will perfect it until the day of Christ Jesus."

Philippians 1:6 NASU

It is written, "THE LORD is my Light and my Salvation — whom shall I fear or dread? The Lord is the Refuge and Stronghold of my life — of whom shall I be afraid? When the wicked, even my enemies and my foes, came upon me to eat up my flesh, they stumbled and fell. Though a host encamp against me, my heart shall not fear; though war arise against me, [even then] in this will I be confident. One thing have I asked of the Lord, that will I seek, inquire for, and [insistently] require: that I may dwell in the house of the Lord [in His presence] all the days of my life, to behold and gaze upon the beauty [the sweet attractiveness and the delightful loveliness] of the Lord and to meditate, consider, and inquire in His temple. For in the day of trouble He will hide me in His shelter; in the secret place of His tent will He hide me; He will set me high upon a rock. And now shall my head be lifted up above my enemies round about me; in His tent I will offer sacrifices and shouting of joy; I will sing, yes, I will sing praises to the Lord. Hear, O Lord, when I cry aloud; have mercy and be gracious to me and answer me! You have said, Seek My face [inquire for and require My presence as your vital need]. My heart says to You, Your face (Your presence), Lord, will I seek, inquire for, and require [of necessity and on the authority of Your Word]. Hide not Your face from me; turn not Your servant away in anger, You Who have been my help! Cast me not off, neither forsake me, O God of my salvation! Although my father and my mother have forsaken me, yet the Lord will take me up [adopt me as His child]. Teach me Your way, O Lord, and lead me in a plain and even path because of my enemies [those who lie in wait for me]. Give me not up to the will of my adversaries, for false witnesses have risen up against me; they breathe out cruelty and violence. [What, what would have become of me] had I not believed that I would see the Lord's goodness in the land of the living! Wait and hope for and expect the Lord; be brave and of good courage and let your heart be stout and enduring. Yes, wait for and hope for and expect the Lord."

Psalm 27:1-14 AMP

It is written, "But those who wait on the Lord shall renew their strength; they shall mount up with wings like eagles, they shall run and not be weary, they shall walk and not faint."

Isaiah 40:31 NKJV

It is written, "For I am persuaded that neither death nor life, nor angels nor principalities nor powers, nor things present nor things to come, nor height nor depth, nor any other created thing, shall be able to separate us from the love of God which is in Christ Jesus our Lord."

Romans 8:38-39 NKJV

It is written, "Do not fear, for I am with you; do not anxiously look about you, for I am your God. I will strengthen you, surely I will help you, surely I will uphold you with My righteous right hand."

Isaiah 41:10 NASU

## CHAPTER 15

# Hope/Peace/ Courage

It is written, "For whatever was written in earlier times was written for our instruction, so that through perseverance and the encouragement of the Scriptures we might have hope."

ROMANS 15:4 NASU

"(As it is written, 'I have made you a father of many nations') in the presence of Him whom he believed — God, who gives life to the dead and calls those things which do not exist as though they did; who, contrary to hope, in hope believed, so that he became the father of many nations, according to what was spoken,

'So shall your descendants be.' And not being weak in faith, he did not consider his own body, already dead (since he was about a hundred years old), and the deadness of Sarah's womb. He did not waver at the promise of God through unbelief, but was strengthened in faith, giving glory to God, and being fully convinced that what He had promised He was also able to perform. And therefore 'It was accounted to him for righteousness.'"

ROMANS 4:17-22 NKJV

It is written, "'For I know the plans that I have for you,' declares the Lord, 'plans for welfare and not for calamity to give you a future and a hope. Then you will call upon Me and come and pray to Me, and I will listen to you. You will seek Me and find Me when you search for Me with all your heart.'"

JEREMIAH 29:11-14 NASU

It is written, "For in hope we have been saved, but hope that is seen is not hope; for who hopes for what he already sees? But if we hope for what we do not see, with perseverance we wait eagerly for it."

Romans 8:24-25 NASU

It is written, "Now faith is the substance of things hoped for, the evidence of things not seen."

Hebrews 11:1 NKJV

It is written, "Blessed is the man who trusts in the Lord, and whose hope is the Lord. For he shall be like a tree planted by the waters, which spreads out its roots by the river,"

Jeremiah 17:7-8 NKJV

It is written, "Hope deferred makes the heart sick, but desire fulfilled is a tree of life."

Proverbs 13:12 NASU

It is written, "These things I have spoken to you, so that in Me you may have peace. In the world you have tribulation, but take courage; I have overcome the world."

JOHN 16:33 NASU

It is written, "You will keep him in perfect peace, whose mind is stayed on You, because he trusts in You. Trust in the Lord forever, for in Yah, the Lord, is everlasting strength."

ISAIAH 26:3-4 NKJV

It is written, "Lord, You will establish peace for us, for You have also done all our works in us."

ISAIAH 26:12 NKJV

It is written, "Peace I leave with you; My peace I give to you; not as the world gives do I give to you. Do not let your heart be troubled, nor let it be fearful."

JOHN 14:27-28 NASU

It is written, "The Lord bless you, and keep you; the Lord make His face shine on you, and be gracious to you; the Lord lift up His countenance on you, and give you peace."

Numbers 6:24-26 NASU

It is written, "Be anxious for nothing, but in everything by prayer and supplication with thanksgiving let your requests be made known to God. And the peace of God, which surpasses all comprehension, will guard your hearts and your minds in Christ Jesus. Finally, brethren, whatever is true, whatever is honorable, whatever is right, whatever is pure, whatever is lovely, whatever is of good repute, if there is any excellence and if anything worthy of praise, dwell on these things. The things you have learned and received and heard and seen in me, practice these things, and the God of peace will be with you."

Philippians 4:6-9 NASU

It is written, "And let the peace of God rule in your hearts, to which also you were called in one body; and be thankful."

Colossians 3:15 NKJV

It is written, "Those who love Your law have great peace, and nothing causes them to stumble."

Psalm 119:165 NASU

It is written, "But now in Christ Jesus you who formerly were far off have been brought near by the blood of Christ. For He Himself is our peace, who made both groups into one and broke down the barrier of the dividing wall, by abolishing in His flesh the enmity, which is the Law of commandments contained in ordinances, so that in Himself He might make the two into one new man, thus establishing peace, and might reconcile them both in one body to God through the cross, by it having put to death the enmity. AND HE CAME AND PREACHED PEACE TO YOU WHO

WERE FAR AWAY, AND PEACE TO THOSE WHO WERE NEAR;"

EPHESIANS 2:13-18 NASU

It is written, "For a child will be born to us, a son will be given to us; and the government will rest on His shoulders; and His name will be called Wonderful Counselor, Mighty God, Eternal Father, Prince of Peace. There will be no end to the increase of His government or of peace, on the throne of David and over his kingdom, to establish it and to uphold it with justice and righteousness from then on and forevermore. The zeal of the Lord of hosts will accomplish this."

ISAIAH 9:6-7 NASU

It is written, "The God of peace will soon crush Satan under your feet."

ROMANS 16:20 NASU

It is written, "In peace I will both lie down and sleep, for You alone, O Lord, make me to dwell in safety."

> Psalm 4:8 NASU

It is written, "The Lord will give strength to His people; the Lord will bless His people with peace."

> Psalm 29:11 NASU

It is written, "Be strong and let your heart take courage, all you who hope in the Lord."

> Psalm 31:24 NASU

It is written, "Have I not commanded you? Be strong and courageous! Do not tremble or be dismayed, for the Lord your God is with you wherever you go."

> Joshua 1:9 NASU

CHAPTER 16

# FREEDOM/ LIBERTY

It is written, "THE SPIRIT OF THE LORD IS UPON ME, BECAUSE HE ANOINTED ME TO PREACH THE GOSPEL TO THE POOR. HE HAS SENT ME TO PROCLAIM RELEASE TO THE CAPTIVES, AND RECOVERY OF SIGHT TO THE BLIND, TO SET FREE THOSE WHO ARE OPPRESSED, TO PROCLAIM THE FAVORABLE YEAR OF THE LORD."

Luke 4:18-19 NASU

It is written, "So Jesus was saying to those Jews who had believed Him, 'If you continue in

My word, then you are truly disciples of Mine; and you will know the truth, and the truth will make you free.' They answered Him, 'We are Abraham's descendants and have never yet been enslaved to anyone; how is it that You say, 'You will become free'?' Jesus answered them, 'Truly, truly, I say to you, everyone who commits sin is the slave of sin. The slave does not remain in the house forever; the son does remain forever. So if the Son makes you free, you will be free indeed.'"

JOHN 8:31-36 NASU

It is written, "It was for freedom that Christ set us free; therefore keep standing firm and do not be subject again to a yoke of slavery."

GALATIANS 5:1 NASU

It is written, "Act as free men, and do not use your freedom as a covering for evil, but use it as bondslaves of God."

1 PETER 2:16-17 NASU

It is written, "Now the Lord is the Spirit, and where the Spirit of the Lord is, there is liberty (emancipation from bondage, freedom)."

2 Corinthians 3:17 AMP

It is written, "Christ purchased our freedom [redeeming us] from the curse (doom) of the Law [and its condemnation] by [Himself] becoming a curse for us, for it is written [in the Scriptures], Cursed is everyone who hangs on a tree (is crucified);"

Galatians 3:13 AMP

It is written, "But when the proper time had fully come, God sent His Son, born of a woman, born subject to [the regulations of] the Law, to purchase the freedom of (to ransom, to redeem, to atone for) those who were subject to the Law, that we might be adopted and have sonship conferred upon us [and be recognized as God's sons]. And because you [really] are [His] sons, God has sent the [Holy] Spirit of

His Son into our hearts, crying, Abba (Father)! Father! Therefore, you are no longer a slave (bond servant) but a son; and if a son, then [it follows that you are] an heir by the aid of God, through Christ."

Galatians 4:4-7 AMP

It is written, "And I will walk at liberty and at ease, for I have sought and inquired for [and desperately required] Your precepts."

Psalm 119:45 AMP

CHAPTER 17

# OVERCOMING TEMPTATION AND ADDICTION

It is written, "Therefore let anyone who thinks he stands [who feels sure that he has a steadfast mind and is standing firm], take heed lest he fall [into sin]. For no temptation (no trial regarded as enticing to sin), [no matter how it comes or where it leads] has overtaken you and laid hold on you that is not common to man [that is, no temptation or trial has come to you that is beyond human resistance and that is not adjusted and adapted and belonging to human experience, and such as man can bear]. But God is faithful [to His Word and to His compassionate nature], and He [can be trusted] not to let you be tempted and tried and assayed beyond your ability and strength of resistance and power to endure, but with the temptation He will [always] also provide the way out (the means of escape to a landing place), that you may be capable and strong and powerful to bear up under it patiently."

1 Corinthians 10:12-13 AMP

It is written, "For sin shall not [any longer] exert dominion over you, since now you are not under Law [as slaves], but under grace [as subjects of God's favor and mercy]."

Romans 6:14 AMP

It is written, "He who covers his sins will not prosper, but whoever confesses and forsakes them will have mercy."

Proverbs 28:13 NKJV

It is written, "So humble yourselves before God. Resist the devil, and he will flee from you. Come close to God, and God will come close to you. Wash your hands, you sinners; purify your hearts, for your loyalty is divided between God and the world. Let there be tears for what you have done. Let there be sorrow and deep grief. Let there be sadness instead of laughter, and gloom instead of joy. Humble yourselves before the Lord, and he will lift you up in honor."

James 4:7-10 NLT

It is written, "But you belong to God, my dear children. You have already won a victory over those people, because the Spirit who lives in you is greater than the spirit who lives in the world. Those people belong to this world, so they speak from the world's viewpoint, and the world listens to them. But we belong to God, and those who know God listen to us. If they do not belong to God, they do not listen to us.

That is how we know if someone has the Spirit of truth or the spirit of deception."

1 John 4:4-6 NLT

It is written, "Inasmuch then as we have a great High Priest Who has [already] ascended and passed through the heavens, Jesus the Son of God, let us hold fast our confession [of faith in Him]. For we do not have a High Priest Who is unable to understand and sympathize and have a shared feeling with our weaknesses and infirmities and liability to the assaults of temptation, but One Who has been tempted in every respect as we are, yet without sinning. Let us then fearlessly and confidently and boldly draw near to the throne of grace (the throne of God's unmerited favor to us sinners), that we may receive mercy [for our failures] and find grace to help in good time for every need [appropriate help and well-timed help, coming just when we need it]."

Hebrews 4:14-16 AMP

It is written, "For in that He Himself has suffered, being tempted, He is able to aid those who are tempted."

Hebrews 2:18 NKJV

It is written, "Then the Lord knows how to deliver the godly out of temptations…"

2 Peter 2:9a NKJV

It is written, "Dear brothers and sisters, when troubles come your way, consider it an opportunity for great joy. For you know that when your faith is tested, your endurance has a chance to grow. So let it grow, for when your endurance is fully developed, you will be perfect and complete, needing nothing. If you need wisdom, ask our generous God, and he will give it to you. He will not rebuke you for asking. But when you ask him, be sure that your faith is in God alone. Do not waver, for a person with divided loyalty is as unsettled as a wave of the sea that is blown and tossed by the wind. Such people should not expect to receive anything from the Lord. Their loyalty is divided between God and the world, and they are unstable in everything they do."

JAMES 1:2-8 NLT

It is written, "God blesses those who patiently endure testing and temptation. Afterward they will receive the crown of life that God has promised to those who love him. And remember, when you are being tempted, do not say, 'God is tempting me.' God is never tempted to do wrong, and he never tempts anyone else. Temptation comes from our own desires, which entice us and drag us away. These desires give birth to sinful actions. And when sin is allowed to grow, it gives birth to death. So don't be misled, my dear brothers and sisters. Whatever is good and perfect comes down to us from God our Father, who created all the lights in the heavens. He never changes or casts a shifting shadow."

JAMES 1:12-18 NLT

It is written, "Now all glory to God, who is able to keep you from falling away and will bring you with great joy into his glorious presence without a single fault. All glory to him who alone is God, our Savior through Jesus Christ our Lord."

Jude 24-25a NLT

It is written, "So be truly glad. There is wonderful joy ahead, even though you have to endure many trials for a little while. These trials will show that your faith is genuine. It is being tested as fire tests and purifies gold—though your faith is far more precious than mere gold. So when your faith remains strong through many trials, it will bring you much praise and glory and honor on the day when Jesus Christ is revealed to the whole world."

1 Peter 1:6-7 NLT

# CHAPTER 18

# Anger

It is written, "But now is the time to get rid of anger, rage, malicious behavior, slander, and dirty language. Don't lie to each other, for you have stripped off your old sinful nature and all its wicked deeds. Put on your new nature, and be renewed as you learn to know your Creator and become like him."

Colossians 3:8-11 NLT

It is written, "You have heard that our ancestors were told, 'You must not murder. If you commit murder, you are subject to judgment.' But I say, if you are even angry with someone, you are subject to judgment!

If you call someone an idiot, you are in danger of being brought before the court. And if you curse someone, you are in danger of the fires of hell. So if you are presenting a sacrifice at the altar in the Temple and you suddenly remember that someone has something against you, leave your sacrifice there at the altar. Go and be reconciled to that person. Then come and offer your sacrifice to God."

MATTHEW 5:21-24 NLT

It is written, "Control your temper, for anger labels you a fool."

ECCLESIASTES 7:9 NLT

It is written, "Understand [this], my beloved brethren. Let every man be quick to hear [a ready listener], slow to speak, slow to take offense and to get angry. For man's anger does not promote the righteousness God [wishes and requires]."

JAMES 1:19-20 AMP

It is written, "This is no light matter. God has warned us that he'll hold us to account and make us pay. He was quite explicit: 'Vengeance is mine, and I won't overlook a thing,' and, 'God will judge his people.' Nobody's getting by with anything, believe me."

Hebrews 10:30-31 MB


It is written, "He who is slow to anger is better than the mighty, he who rules his [own] spirit than he who takes a city."

Proverbs 16:32 AMP


It is written, "Stop being angry! Turn from your rage! Do not lose your temper—it only leads to harm."

Psalm 37:8 NLT


It is written, "Dear friends, never take revenge. Leave that to the righteous anger of God. For the Scriptures say, 'I will take revenge; I will pay them back,' says the Lord. Instead, 'If your enemies are hungry, feed them. If they are thirsty, give them something to drink. In doing this, you will heap burning coals of shame on their heads.' Don't let evil conquer you, but conquer evil by doing good."

Romans 12:19-21 NLT

It is written, "When angry, do not sin; do not ever let your wrath (your exasperation, your fury or indignation) last until the sun goes down. Leave no [such] room or foothold for the devil [give no opportunity to him]."

Ephesians 4:26-27 AMP

It is written, "Let all bitterness, wrath, anger, clamor, and evil speaking be put away from you, with all malice. And be kind to one another, tenderhearted, forgiving one another, even as God in Christ forgave you."

Ephesians 4:31-32 NKJV

It is written, "The wise watch their steps and avoid evil; fools are headstrong and reckless. The hotheaded do things they'll later regret; the coldhearted get the cold shoulder."

Proverbs 14:16-17 MB

It is written, "A gentle answer deflects anger, but harsh words make tempers flare."

Proverbs 15:1 NLT

It is written, "People with understanding control their anger; a hot temper shows great foolishness."

Proverbs 14:29 NLT

It is written, "A hot-tempered man stirs up strife, but the slow to anger calms a dispute."

Proverbs 15:18 NASU

It is written, "If you forgive those who sin against you, your heavenly Father will forgive you. But if you refuse to forgive others, your Father will not forgive your sins."

Matthew 6:14-15 NLT

It is written, "The Lord is compassionate and merciful, slow to get angry and filled with unfailing love."

Psalm 103:8 NLT

It is written, "Don't sin by letting anger control you. Think about it overnight and remain silent."

Psalm 4:4 NLT

It is written, "Good sense makes a man restrain his anger, and it is his glory to overlook a transgression or an offense."

Proverbs 19:11 AMP

It is written, "Scorners set a city aflame, but wise men turn away anger."

Proverbs 29:8 NASU

# CHAPTER 19

# Love

It is written, "If I speak with the tongues of men and of angels, but do not have love, I have become a noisy gong or a clanging cymbal. If I have the gift of prophecy, and know all mysteries and all knowledge; and if I have all faith, so as to remove mountains, but do not have love, I am nothing. And if I give all my possessions to feed the poor, and if I surrender my body to be burned, but do not have love, it profits me nothing. Love is patient, love is kind and is not jealous; love does not brag and is not arrogant, does not act unbecomingly; it does not seek its own, is not provoked, does not take into account a wrong suffered, does not rejoice in unrighteousness, but rejoices with the truth; bears all things, believes all things, hopes all things, endures all things. Love never fails ... But now faith, hope, love, abide these three; but the greatest of these is love."

1 Corinthians 13:1-8a; 13 NASU

It is written, "But in all these things we overwhelmingly conquer through Him who loved us. For I am convinced that neither death, nor life, nor angels, nor principalities, nor things present, nor things to come, nor powers, nor height, nor depth, nor any other created thing, will be able to separate us from the love of God, which is in Christ Jesus our Lord."

Romans 8:38-39 NASU

It is written, "The person who has My commands and keeps them is the one who [really] loves Me; and whoever [really] loves Me will be loved by My Father, and I [too] will love him and will show (reveal, manifest)

Myself to him. [I will let Myself be clearly seen by him and make Myself real to him.]"

John 14:21 AMP

It is written, "Beloved, let us love one another, for love is from God; and everyone who loves is born of God and knows God. The one who does not love does not know God, for God is love. By this the love of God was manifested in us, that God has sent His only begotten Son into the world so that we might live through Him. In this is love, not that we loved God, but that He loved us and sent His Son to be the propitiation for our sins. Beloved, if God so loved us, we also ought to love one another. No one has seen God at any time; if we love one another, God abides in us, and His love is perfected in us."

1 John 4:7-12 NASU

It is written, "All who confess that Jesus is the Son of God have God living in them, and they live in God. We know how much God loves us, and we have put our trust in his love. God is love, and all who live in love live in God, and God lives in them. And as we live in God, our love grows more perfect. So we will not be afraid on the day of judgment, but we can face him with confidence because we live like Jesus here in this world. Such love has no fear, because perfect love expels all fear. If we are afraid, it is for fear of punishment, and this shows that we have not fully experienced his perfect love. We love each other because he loved us first. If someone says, "I love God," but hates a Christian brother or sister, that person is a liar; for if we don't love people we can see, how can we love God, whom we cannot see? And he has given us this command: Those who love God must also love their Christian brothers and sisters."

1 John 4:15-21 NLT

It is written, "And you shall love the Lord your God with all your heart, with all your soul, with all your mind, and with all your strength.' This is the first commandment. And the second, like it, is this: 'You shall love your neighbor as yourself.' There is no other commandment greater than these."

Mark 12:30-31 NKJV

It is written, "But God demonstrates His own love toward us, in that while we were still sinners, Christ died for us."

Romans 5:8-9 NKJV

It is written, "For God so loved the world that He gave His only begotten Son, that whoever believes in Him should not perish but have everlasting life."

John 3:16 NKJV

It is written, "I pray that from his glorious, unlimited resources he will empower you with inner strength through his Spirit. Then Christ will make his home in your hearts as you trust in him. Your roots will grow down into God's love and keep you strong. And may you have the power to understand, as all God's people should, how wide, how long, how high, and how deep his love is. May you experience the love of Christ, though it is too great to understand fully. Then you will be made complete with all the fullness of life and power that comes from God."

Ephesians 3:16-19 NLT

It is written, "Just as the Father has loved Me, I have also loved you; abide in My love. If you keep My commandments, you will abide in My love; just as I have kept My Father's commandments and abide in His love."

John 15:9-10 NASU

It is written, "This is My commandment, that you love one another, just as I have loved you. Greater love has no one than this, that one lay down his life for his friends. You are My friends if you do what I command you ... This I command you, that you love one another."

JOHN 15:12-14; 17 NASU

It is written, "A new commandment I give to you, that you love one another, even as I have loved you, that you also love one another. By this all men will know that you are My disciples, if you have love for one another."

JOHN 13:34-35 NASU

# ABOUT THE AUTHOR

Rhonda grew up in rural Missouri and graduated from Ottawa University in Overland Park, Kansas, and has had a dedicated, compassionate career in the healthcare industry. She has served in many different roles of ministry in the local church but is best known for her teaching and prayer ministry. Rhonda's first book, *Road to Transformation, Journey to God's Glory*, was released in 2014. Since then, she launched the Christian teaching blog Secret Place Revelation, inspired by Psalm 91:1, "He that dwelleth in the secret place of the most High shall abide under the shadow of the Almighty." In 2017, her second book, *Keys to the Kingdom* was released. Rhonda is passionate about sharing the truths of God's Word and enjoys speaking in many settings and teaching small groups.

To contact Rhonda, please visit:
www.secretplacerevelation.com
or email rhondabarnes@embarqmail.com.

# Note from the Publisher

## Are you a first time author?

Not sure how to proceed to get your book published?
Want to keep all your rights and all your royalties?
Want it to look as good as a Top 10 publisher?
Need help with editing, layout, cover design?
Want it out there selling in 90 days or less?

## Visit our website for some exciting new options!

www.chalfant-eckert-publishing.com

Made in the USA
Columbia, SC
31 August 2017